PERFECT BLUE

Kona Macphee was born in London and grew up in Australia, where she worked as a waitress, shop assistant and apprentice motorbike mechanic. She studied musical composition at the Sydney Conservatorium, violin at the University of Sydney, and computer science and robotics at Monash University, later taking an M.Sc. at Cambridge as a Commonwealth Scholar. She received an Eric Gregory Award for her poetry in 1998, and has published two collections with Bloodaxe, *Tails* (2004) and *Perfect Blue* (2010). She is a freelance writer and software developer, and lives in Crieff, Perthshire.

KONA MACPHEE'S WEBSITE: www.konamacphee.com
For additional material relating to the poems in this book, including recordings and commentaries, see: www.konamacphee.com/pb/

KONA MACPHEE

Perfect Blue

BLOODAXE BOOKS

Copyright © Kona Macphee 2010

ISBN: 978 1 85224 866 6

First published 2010 by
Bloodaxe Books Ltd,
Highgreen,
Tarset,
Northumberland NE48 1RP.

www.bloodaxebooks.com
For further information about Bloodaxe titles
please visit our website or write to
the above address for a catalogue.

Supported by
ARTS COUNCIL
ENGLAND

Cover design: Neil Astley & Pamela Robertson-Pearce.

Printed in Great Britain by
Bell & Bain Limited, Glasgow, Scotland.

For old ways and new beginnings

ACKNOWLEDGEMENTS

Acknowledgements are due to the following publications, in which some of these poems first appeared: *Acumen*, www. booksfromscotland.com, *The Golden Hour Book: Volume II* (Forest Publications, 2009), *Identity Parade: New British & Irish Poets* (Bloodaxe Books, 2010), *Magma, New Welsh Review, Northwords Now* and *Poetry Wales*.

CONTENTS

II

PERFECT BLUE

I

Iubilate

Laden as they were with plastic bags
of all the usual crap they harvested
and carted home, enmazed

within the polished, repetitious panes
of shop displays tricked up like sideshow mirrors
to proffer different selves,

not one amongst the weekend shoppers raised
their eyes beyond that retail paradise
into the vaulted space

above the Main Arcade, where one lone pane
of perspex near the Starbucks end revealed
a colouring of sky

unmired by moss, or weathering, or grime,
a rectangle of clarity restored
last Monday night in haste –

after he scaled the multistorey stairs
to summit on the walled perimeter
of Carpark Level Ten,

chanced a long breath, then with a look uncaught
on CCTV footage, slung himself
onto the cold spring day –

that sloped pane where his arching plummet touched
the margins of the closed-up shoppers' world:
now glossed, immaculate,

as though a fleet of ghostly seraphim
had trailed his fall with bitter iubilates
and now were sealed below

to buff forever with their panicked wings
that gleaming surface, trying to regain
the endless, perfect blue.

The invention of the electric chair

All the slow purposes that make a tree
were in you once – to grow; to gauge
in every measured angle of your leaves
that moving target, light; to hold
through winter like an indrawn breath; to feel
the buzz of resurrection borne on spring.

As neutral wood suborns to dark intents
of blame, in icons hewn and nailed –
the scaffold and the catherine wheel,
the cross and gallows: symbols of
a skill that's more than carpentry,
and deeply less than human – so, lost tree,

this timber rictus of your supple green
has made a foursquare chair. Now history
awaits in thrall the painted scene
that might beatify your sacrifice –
those drooping limbs surrendered to your arms;
that smoking moment held: a Pietà.

Addiction

Frost in the air, all naked metal cold
and grippy; travellers hunker egglike and unwarmed
in cracking plastic shelters, waiting
for the last bus here or there to wheeze them
home in a haze of diesel and fatigue.

Around the back, graffiti's restless verdancy
blooms and fades, blooms and fades; the smell
of half-drunk Special Brews and pissed-up walls
thickens to near-visible around the toilet block,
its entrance like a single poked-out eye

behind which, in the grime-encrypted light,
a tremor nearly casts the opened powder
down to the mud-streaked puddle of the floor.
More often now, the flagging body manifests
these sudden shorthand fallibilities,

each coding nothing more than *not enough*
or ghosting an unspoken wish – that once,
just once, the hurt biology that dares
the knife-edged balance of a dose might slip
and tumble, manumitted, to the glory side,

might drop away, forget this after-image
(a prick-marked husk of cold blue flesh, cast off
and hollow like a perfect insect casing
left for the dawnshift cleaners to reveal) –
but not tonight. At this unhallowed hour

what mercy falls, falls sparsely, haltingly,
like juddered breath or the hard fluorescence
stuttering over the oil-sheened road
from the failing tube at Bargain Hunters' Heaven:
a fumble is averted; a vein does not collapse;

pain lessens. Now the final chilly straggler
boards at last the closing Number Thirty.
Across the clear-skied coldness of the town,
a starched cathedral cancels its assurances;
the pinned moon suffers on its pointed spire.

Wild night's morning

Watch, as storm-lees
settle in the air,
a black rood, pendant,
mullioning a square

of cloud-merled sky:
one crow, athwart
the erratic wind,
and an omen caught

in his own mischance
(fox-struck, cat-nipped
or weather-strafed?):
one pinion stripped

to a chancel-lattice
or the ragged fringe
of a roof subsiding;
yet look – he'll hinge

on that half-plumed wing
and hold his course,
annul each gust
with accordant force:

the metaphor
in his ruined grace
not a sundered abbey
but a boxer's face.

Pheasant and astronomers
(for GTR)

Burnished, finicky, picking his headbob way
across the asphalt path, into the leafy scrub
behind the twelve-pane window of our office,

we can't not watch his colours in the sunlight.
Our measures and projections fall aside
as coarsest calculus to his most perfect curve;

so we observe.
             Can such a day-star brave
the midnight sky whose glaring spectral eyes
seethe down the invert shrinkage of a telescope,

or does he sleep all clouded in the hedgerows'
straight-line rays of green restraint to roads
that sling his slow kin cockeyed in the gutter?

On foot and unconcerned, he patters out of view,
out of our world again; the sunlit room
falls just a lumen dimmer with his passing.

The short answer

At fourteen miles per second, a simple fleck of paint
could punch a hole in you the likes of which
Jet Li would hardly credit. Consider hunting down

each mote of dust or skin that's floating in this room,
then tracking its meanderings for ever:
that's what it's like up there, where every dot of mass

in orbit must be plotted, where a misplaced spanner's
no mere irritation, but a debt
of slipped attention doomed to endless interest; so

it's fortunate for us things move at measured pace
down here, and tend to linger where we drop them;
thus, objects that would waltz away in zero-G,

their glinting arms extended, waving last goodbyes,
instead stay where they were: in other words,
my dearest, no, I don't know where your car keys are.

A year in the back country

By winter it was all we had –
a thin sense of ourselves that clung
like stale smoke, or a papery veneer
of grained oak over chipboard.
The wave of fizzing verve that filled
our cabin to its rafters at the start
had drained, and now we crossed the floor
on wooden legs, through silt. I could have
murdered for a burger, or a TV ad –
some brightly-wrapped vacuity
to leaven that relentless depth,
to hint of levels sunlight reached –
but no, we floundered onward, drawn
by little glows of promise: hope;
a pallid wish to be transformed;
the sense that *something* had to happen
soon; our rigid pride. We only saw
the snag-toothed brutes who played these lures
too late: that day (our faces glazed,
our heads refracting knotty tats
of warm-beast-smelling hair), when Sophie
came to bring us home, approaching
eagerly at first, and then
(as we sat wordless on the stoop,
a strange electric hum behind
our blanked-off eyes) more warily,
until she paused, quite silent, and
began to back away, then turned and ran,
and we sprang up in concord, not
to follow but pursue, each knowing
just how far the other man would go.

Self-portrait aged 8 with electric fence

I steeled myself
and touched the wire:
it turned my hand
from flesh to fire,

my nerves to spark,
my muscles, rock,
my arm a spike
of hard white shock –

and now I reach
for words that sound
each arc of hurt
from hand to ground.

Pears Translucent Soap

The smell is warm bath, wet clean hair
and just being small, the feel
of rough towel reaching neck to floor
and hem to spare. I wrap

my arms around themselves to hold
that littleness, that brittle
not-quite-memory until
the shower rains it gone,

then lift the glassy soap again:
here's fingers trapped in amber,
tenderness and slap a hundred
million years away – and here's

that achy smell once more. I wish –
but no, I will not wish. Instead,
I rinse my face. The water strikes
or strokes my cheek; I can't decide.

To a young daughter

Sore as the sorest thumb you think
you're sticking out like, clubbed today
by differentness, cut off, left out,
I'd fold you up in ugly-duckling
promises of future perfect

sisterhood revealed, but then
I think of swans, those debutantes
who grace the loch in glossed parade –
that brutal elegance, that blank
exactitude! – and I recall

instead the mountain hare, whose pelt
pulsates with light and dark, a beat
that's metered by her essence, not
the world's erratic seasons; who,
beneath a mild December sky

(no snow to coat the bog-black peat,
to smooth the stalky heather), finds
herself a radiant dissident,
her bluewhite glow a lonely vote
for somewhere else's winter. Spied,

she freezes in a bid to fade
that's doomed by what she is; and yet
she lives; she fears and lives, preserves
her only self, that soon the world
must answer her with snow.

Autumn evening blues

Love, as the day's length plummets
down the shot-tower fall of October
and this old house is reminded
of its standing invitation to the cold,

remember this: the chilled skin warms
by inner-dwelling heat; our eyes
in common darkness barely glimmer,
yet burn like tigers in the infrared.

Justice

Does it lie
on a soft pillow, in cleanest laundered sheets,
history's yellow newspapers crammed beneath the mattress?

Is it cut
in the ritual, careless combat of the courts,
in the presidential veto, the filibustered vote?

Can it live
in the breath between righteous, angry heartbeats,
in the little voids between opposing teeth?

Might it hide
in the small arms of child soldiers
allowed at last to leave the heavy guns?

Will it speak
in the broadcast soundbites of a far rebellion,
or an inward, partisan murmur of forgiveness?

Newsbites

These conflicts always stem from faith or race.
(Subtitle: Leading Academic's views.)
[Now cut to close-up; linger on ravaged face.]

There's fear the growing violence might displace
the farmers, with their yearly crop to lose.
These conflicts always stem from faith or race.

Another bombing struck the marketplace
this morning, near the long employment queues.
[Now cut to close-up; linger on ravaged face.]

The children here have vanished without trace.
[Slow pan across a blood-stained pile of shoes.]
These conflicts always stem from faith or race.

The overflowing camps have no more space
for victims trickling back in ones and twos.
[Now cut to close-up; linger on ravaged face.]

The ceasefire holds, but nothing can erase
the painful memories. More in tomorrow's news.
These conflicts always stem from faith or race.
[Now cut to close-up; linger on ravaged face.]

Wildwar

a barrage cracks above a crouching rat

a toad's fat ambush smacks a rolling tank

a beetle gambles on the air's hot roulette

a tracer fires an owl to fleeting phoenix

a moth's course grazes a swollen cheek of smoke

a heat-scorched seed-head forfeits all its knowledge

a house-mouse whiskers in the rubble's brutal maze

a dogged rose prepares its shreds of flowers

Exit hymn

From the fouled sea when the last ice
thins to nil, a parting wave will surge
and pound regret in freights of heavy metals

> *praise sea, the green sea, by whose grace*
> *the mad chance of the prototypes*
> *of every living cell could speculate*

From the wan earth when the spring shrugs,
a trillion shoots of penitence will rise,
their palm-frond fingers blackening to ash

> *praise earth, the fair earth, by whose grace*
> *the slow blast of the bursting seed*
> *extends for decades, flaring out a tree*

From the smirched air when the last bird
falls unflighted, vengeful winds will swell
and howl their helpless judgement in the valleys

> *praise air, the clear air, by whose grace*
> *the wet sacks of our lungs beget*
> *their flow of gifts, each one another breath*

From the vast fire when the sun seethes
will come a cleansing rage to simplify
all form to matter, strewn, innocent

> *praise sun, the wild sun, by whose grace*
> *all graces issue, by whose end*
> *all endings are undone: o praise the sun*

The problem of the bees

Inside the templed city, writers tend
the stone-walled gardens of their cleverness,
and flaunt them, with the air of pioneers
who think they've mapped the limits of the west,

at scientists who know they have unpicked
the bumblebee's enigma, and henceforth
can mount it, dead and labelled, on a pin
which, dropped in water, turns and wavers north

to where, far off, an ageing canvas, stretched
and mounted in the manner of the east,
is ever blank, despite the fecund brush
the artist borrowed from the orchidist,

while up and down the country, thrumming hives
fall silent overnight – and in the south,
a skein of pollen rides the wind beyond
the apple-blossom's parched and begging mouth.

THE BOOK OF DISEASES

Leprosy

Even the merest millionth part of blood
attracts the polished sensor of a shark;
the rubbery planet of a whale detects
a finger-tip's most transitory arc –

yet sense can lie (the elephant became
to six blind men a pillar and a rope,
a branch, a waving fan, a wall, a pipe;
the anorexic sees a different shape) –

and sense can be deceived (the phantom limb;
the dentist's prick of novocaine that stings
a cheek to swollen blubber, muted, bland;
the stage magician's dextrous conjuring) –

and sense can even die – imagine this:
to watch as tunnel-vision burrows in;
to hear, like Ludwig, music's dying fall;
to touch and not to feel another skin.

Scarlet fever

In the office, the slender plot-lines on the charts
conspire to veer the wrong way, down, and cross the border
into the rough terrain of in-the-red. Now heads
will roll, he knows, and of course it's always the footsoldiers first,
no matter how loyal and true, how many years they've served.

On the 5:20 home, his mercury's rising again:
he curses the plague of the mobile phone, and in his mind
the stubby handset clutched by Mister I'M ON THE TRAIN
a few rows down spontaneously explodes, takes out
that oafish head, and all admire the smashed remains,
the lovely splash of scarlet on the window pane.

This evening his wife's indifferent back in bed is turned
to him, a bracket round the start of private thoughts.
He sleeps a while, then waking sweaty from bad dreams,
he doesn't sleep. The embery glow of digits on
their squat clock-radio engulfs the corner of
the room, as though a private hatch to hell were waiting
open behind the bedside drawers: a crimson light
in the dark might be a guiding beacon or a warning –
it all depends on whether you know how lost you are.

Pleurisy

Tighter, Bowen; draw those laces in!
Apply your knee – just so – if you require it.

That nanny, Squires – you must have heard the name
in backstairs gossip – came when I was eight,
replacing Maher, and stayed five years to tend us.
I'm sure Papa had reasons of his own,
most excellent, for placing her, but still
those days were dark. I was not sad today
to hear the whispered news of her departure
from our lives to the next. I hope she rests
in perfect peace and far from any children.

No, no! – to pluck like that's no use! Apply
a forceful tug. You have done this before?

When I was ten, my brother Tom and I
contracted pleurisy – he swiftly died,
as you may know, which heartbroke poor Mama
(her firstborn son! That golden angel gone!)
I was too ill to see his burial,
but heard the nurse being told of how she swooned
beside his little plot, was carried home
and took herself at once to her darkened room.
Maternal visits to the nursery ceased
for many weeks; my sickbed, too, she found
she could not bear, so heavy was her loss.

Pass me that measure there – now see, we have
an inch at least remaining at the waist.

Of course, I mourned dear Tom, but could not cry:
the desperate constriction of my lungs
prevented all exertion, even grief.
I mourned him, but in truth, that sickroom spell
was not unpleasant: spring came to the world,
birdsong and muted sunshine stealing entry
about the careless guard of drawn-in curtains;
the nurse was kind, though chattered much of nothing,
and Squires, disdaining illness, kept away.

That's very good – we almost have it now –
so do take care! – you must preserve the tension.

Best of all, though, dear Papa vouchsafed
a nightly visit, and scarcely missed it once.
I loved his warm tobacco smell, his voice
enquiring gently after my health that day,
his noble profile. (How I wished he'd scoop me
out of that bed, and steal me off to share
the masculine force and mystery of his life!)
I saw him in those convalescent weeks
more frequently than ever before, or since...
but how I prattle on! That was the past,
and it, like Squires, is over with and gone.

My breath confronts the whalebone's strict embrace.
That's perfect, Bowen. Tie the laces off.

Gonorrhoea

Today, a mass assembly in the camp
before we get our bromide-tasting tea;
the visiting colonel scolds us, once again:
A military offence to get VD!

We stand in ordered silence for a while,
then Private Fenton, ever the lig, exclaims
Will we be clapped in irons, sir?, is sent
straight back to front-line duty for his pains.

Thus discipline and hygiene are restored;
tomorrow, another virgin soldier falls,
and Private Fenton claps his hands around
the shrapnel-wound that used to be his balls.

Depression

the mind pursues
a witless grind
beneath this caul
of lethargy

its constant mate
a fleet of thoughts
that race unchecked
but never free

until the day
(so sweet, so far)
when earth rains down
to lift from me

this brain, its choke
of branching veins,
exchange them for
a stone, a tree

Influenza

Senators, here is my report: the ship
descended into orbit a month ago,
the lander made earthfall two days later.
Naturally, the matter has been handled discreetly;
there has been no mention in the public broadcasts.

Return. O tiny beacon, blue gleam
whirling on a fragile thread of gravity,
first mothership, tangible memory!
That delicate glow, your wrap of atmosphere,
leaches promise to the permeating dark.

The historical archives have been combed
for any mention of their ship, their remit:
the mission's origins remain unknown,
and thus, we assume, pre-date the Great Redemption
when records, as you know, were purified.

What we have touched with our seven senses!
The dark sheets pegged between the pendant stars,
the infinite pinprick of a galaxy's heart,
the joyful wild diversity of planets:
our purpose is fulfilled a millionfold.

Senators, I warn you, we must not be complacent.
There's a strangeness…those people are no longer ours.
Something out there has left them changed,
alarming, enigmatic, entirely unpredictable:
we see no hope of proper Integration.

Our selves are a journey's chronicle, a legend
lived, a narration of all that we have seen.
We move as ants, so many and yet one,
knowing that time is a Möbius ribbon
on which we travel, no beginning, without end.

Since their arrival, one has fallen ill
with pain, lethargy, weakness and fever –
a grave condition unknown to our medics.
The records speak of an ancient disease
to which, it seems, they no longer have immunity.

After so long, Earth's lambency of life,
glowing, flickering, such cornucopic brilliance!
The tiniest virus is a miracle spark
flaring on the galaxy's slow entropic embers:
filling us with rhapsody, with awe, with love.

And so, the voyagers are indefinitely contained
(entirely, of course, for their own protection)
in our best Correctional Medicine facility.
They are kept under watch, but senators, in truth
one can't help feel that they are watching us.

In these blank-walled cubes, half-drowning in false light,
our flower-faces track the hidden drift of stars,
our filamentious selves reach softly to each other,
to all the others, everywhere exalting:
o brothers, sisters, glory and rejoice.

Plague

They track the vector to a coastal town
in the south of France, chock-full
of grifters and dysphoric millionaires;
that grey face hasn't aged, nor eased
its malfeasance of angles to put on
a less inhuman mien – but, as ever,
cash, that mighty leveller, gussies up
his oddest semblances as just a splash
of quasi-local colour, blotting out
the quibbles, the uneases;

while back in Kensington – that world
where simpler ugliness might be elided
by pedigrees and pre-nups – a jilted bride
ponders his leavings: another eldest son
of an eldest son now shucking off
the final casings of his privilege
to come up clean, his new eyes green
and hard as emerald marbles, overglazed
with all the fervour of the novice damned
to spread affliction, and to fall redeemed.

Dysentery

The moment of revelation? It arrived
three weeks, two days into the jungle fieldwork;
twelve days after he found the unmapped village;
four days beyond the lamented instant when
he lost his footing in the chest-high river, lost
the bag that he'd been porting on his head
that held, with other things, the lighter, stove,
and purifying gear (but not, thank god,
his little luxury – the suede-bound notebook
embossed with his initials, now half-filled
with weeks of notes and pompous observations:
'the life is spartan here, and brutal too',
'they have so little, and waste nothing', yet
'they seem surprisingly content – resigned?');
three days from when the sickness first began.

The moment came at morning when, exhausted
from keeping nothing in or down, too weak
to stand, and lost in fantasy (a pack
of triple-thickness toilet roll, its wrap
of plastic peeled with reverence like the skin
of some expensive fruit, its velvet sheets
in cream, or peach, embossed with fleurs-de-lys) –
precisely when his shaking hand reached out
and slipped the suede-bound notebook from his pack,
caressed a cartridge page, with one thought: *paper*.

That was the moment: and the last two days,
nothing could wipe the smile off his face.

Typhoid

(for the women of Long Grove)

here she is that one
open face no-mask one
white clothes always a smile
the sometimes one hug one

bringing tray food tea
a picture book such colours
bright in my room
my white always room

spoon tinking in the tea
boiling hot goes round
toilet boiling round and round
and round and gone

she says june again june
and her long long days
longing for what? so gone
blond curls baby smell

tea there was a kitchen
making tea me a man
loud warm hands laughing
children table round and round

perhaps today she says
perhaps they'll come today
those birds she means
I'm sure those birds again

outside my window round
and round when day goes
down those birds go round
like water draining

spinning little spinners
mother made for me
squared paper and a pin
blowing them around

around the cake the years
come round and round again
gone then I was gone
who helped my babies blow?

no cake today rice pudding
brown curl thin jam
eat it up now good girl
eat it up all gone

I'm sick aren't I
I say to her sick
my hand her hand stroking
old skin round and round

just smiles sad eyes
get a little round
doesn't hurt now I say
it's all gone

Smallpox

the desert snake who oscillates
behind a zoo-tank's static waterfall
of safety glass, the urge
to ply his golden strike asleep
but stirring in his flicker and his sway

the spiderling who meditates
upon the beetle in his silken caul
that quivers on the verge
of stillness, innards ripening for the reap:
the children shudder, but they let him stay

the scorpion who calibrates
his captured sting against a jar's smooth wall
as though we might converge
on the opinion, stated in his creep,
that he is predator, his captors, prey

the arrow frog who scintillates
within a careful leafweave basket, all
his focus on the surge
that waits to launch his body in a leap
and put those poisoned colours on display

the virus that perpetuates
a memory of smallpox, phialled recall
of pestilence, of scourge:
another pretty danger that we keep
just close enough, just far enough away

Cholera

Pyotr Ilyich Tchaikovsky, d. 6 November 1893

From the final, faultless premiere
(those rich necks chilled by his swansong Sixth,
that *requiescat* quaking the trombones),
the portents swelled in crescendo premonition:

the dinners with old friends; the creamy taper
of his last baton, laid to its satined bed
like the long shank of a pale and lovely boy;

the subtle prescience of future crowds
whose ghostly tribute massed on Nevsky Prospect;

the secret life in a clear glass of water.

Syphilis
Al Capone in three manifestations

Primary: New York

What was the first site of the infection?
Was it his beefy face, the slashed left side
he turns away in photos? Something else is marred
by scars he paints in not-quite-outright lies

as war wounds, but not anything
the Five Points Gang would recognise; besides,
what prickly truth could vaccinate against
the dark concealed beneath the underground?

Secondary: Cicero

Within the gilded fortress of the Lexington Hotel,
no skin will speckle with the backspat residues
of gunfire, rented muscle will not flex,
blood will not spill, unless he orders it.

Outside, there's jazz and moonshine flaring up
in speakeasies: contagious rhythm, bouts
of drunkenness and whoring. There are bars
that no-one sees, but everybody knows.

Tertiary: Alcatraz

In Cicero, a page of winter snow might blot
the ledger of the streets, collude in brief
with whitewash and denial, filling in
the bullet-pock stigmata, sheeting-over sin;

but here in Frisco Bay there's just a fog
that rolls in from the sea and hangs
a muggy drape of bafflement: at last
he's fingered by the one that got away.

Epilogue

Your span's prescribed by hands unknown;
as to the rest, you're on your own.
The time is nigh, the hour is close:
you won't exceed the stated dose.

NOTES

Leprosy: Damage to peripheral nerves, resulting loss of sensation, is common in leprosy.

Gonorrhoea: WW2 British troops believed that bromide was added to their tea to suppress their libidos. Gonorrhoea is also known as 'the clap'.

Typhoid: It is possible to be an asymptomatic carrier of typhoid. According to the BBC, between 1907 and 1992 a number of female carriers were detained for life in Long Grove mental asylum, Surrey, not because they were ill or insane but simply to prevent them spreading the disease. Many of them were married women with children. The toilets in their building apparently flushed with boiling water.

Smallpox: The World Health Organisation declared in 1979 that the human viral disease smallpox had been wholly eradicated from the world. Officially, only two reserves of the smallpox virus remain in existence, in research labs in Russia and the US. There has been much debate about whether these should be destroyed or preserved.

Cholera: Pyotr Ilyich Tchaikovsky died nine days after conducting the first performance of his final symphony, the Pathetique, and apparently from cholera (which was active at the time in St Petersburg). The circumstances of his death remain controversial, and some suggest that he committed suicide by deliberately drinking unboiled, contaminated water. He was a covert and apparently tormented homosexual.

Syphilis: It is alleged that the gangster Al Capone contracted syphilis in his early life, and that mental confusion in his last years was due to the tertiary phase of the disease.

PERFECT BLUE

II

The detour

They miss the side-road that he'd spoken of,
that storm-haired man two towns back in the bar,
the track that meets the road that leaves the highway –
or so they guess, when – surely! – too far on,
they find a track on the unexpected side
that almost nicks the road, once, and again,
then founders at a rusted-open gate.

Is this the one he meant? she says; he shrugs,
wishing she hadn't asked. He doesn't know.
Why don't we try to ask someone? she adds
as always, but the usual feud's forestalled
by pithy fact: she *can't* have failed to notice
they haven't passed a farm, a house, a barn,
even a goddamn car in twenty miles.

The hire car's sat-nav screen shows near-precisely
the nowhere that they're in the middle of,
but one key detail's lost – the track's not there,
and when they ease unsurely past the gateposts
(*just to take a look,* and *not too far!*),
the navigation console's so offended
it ceases to work at all, and sulks *No signal.*

They follow the track's loose curves along a ridgeside,
their wake a dust-snake lingering in the air
unnervingly: it hisses *They went this way.*
She fidgets, cranes to look behind; he stares
two feet ahead to dodge the frequent potholes,
and if the landscape's growing a little strange,
they're too concerned with what they'll find to notice.

Then suddenly *To the right!* she shrills, *The building!*
He looks along her jolting finger's cue
(the car, too, drifting rightwards), *Where? Where is it?*,
and thus he fails to miss the dust-filled crater
(knee-deep, at least) that grounds the front suspension,
graunches it up again with a rending shriek
of metal bent or broken, leaves it seized.

What do they know of cars? Well, just this much:
there's no way this one's going any further.
They both draw breath, as if they might commence
remonstrances: but no, the moment passes.
The *Shed? House? Factory?* she thought she saw?
Where is it? – I don't know! I'm sure I saw it.
Their cellphones find no signal: dead as bricks.

The car's a dust-pied bubble of denial:
the cup-holders, the sheeny wood-veneer,
the fancy luggage murmuring *luxury*.
Suspended in the blond faux-leather seats
they stare from faced-off windows. Now, at last,
they notice the meagre vegetation's oddness,
its nasty tendrils quivering on the breeze.

The sun is going down, though by their reckoning
it's still mid-afternoon: their watches, phones
and dashboard all claim wildly different times.
A tremulous foreboding builds around them,
but only reaches panic when she whimpers
This isn't what he said it would be like,
and just for once, he entirely agrees.

Three vagaries

I

Two hours' too little sleep:
I sit and contemplate the wilting pot
of all my green intentions.

II

A fly explores this map
of nowhere on the dry back of my hand;
blood pools in silted deltas.

III

After the curtain falls
our scene shifts left, then rolls on in the wings,
unwatched, unscripted, dazzling.

Borrowdale

All night the sound of river:
the plummet-splash of little rapids,
rustling hems of water-skirted rock.

At morning, breakfast: faces pour
their streams of snapshots, every one
so nearly like the last.

Fen train

a flock of swans, unshepherded,
grazes the chocolate soil,
their poise recalling long-drained meres
from which this ground was thieved

small runnels hold their stringent course
in high-walled ersatz banks,
while all around them, chastened peats
subdue themselves yet lower

the fencelines sketch geometries:
a rhombus, ploughed, and here
a box of ponies hunched in rugs,
their withers to the wind

now we take flight against a race
of pylons held in yoke
by rhythmical catenaries
that sag, swoop upwards, sag

then canted roofs of warehouses,
half-empty business parks,
a crammed pragmatic town, its new-builds'
vacant symmetries

now fields again, as rain makes slants
against the pane, defies
the dogged level of the land,
the blurred horizon's rule

to which each poplar perpendicts
its verticality –
a leafless plumbline to some star
the transient whoopers know

whose beacon spark might bode a tide
that comes to sink these rails,
these roads, these fields, reclaim this world
for water, wind and sky

The malfunction

Arriving in good time, it all turned bad:
the last train missed on empty Platform Three.
The closed ranks of the station clocks advanced
in massed reproach, well in advance of me.

My watch had gained the knack of losing time,
not every day, or even every week,
but now and then a gout of minutes gone,
a sudden gush, a splash, a spill, a leak.

Just once, I caught the damn thing in the act:
the second hand, relentless to the last,
was ticking off its usual dogged arc –
but anticlockwise, back into the past.

If only its dictatorship could reach
beyond my wrist, to drive reality
in brief reverse – the contretemps repaired,
the chances seized, the possibilities!

I know time's arrow, river, one-way street
moves ever onward, cannot be defied
by one rebellious gadget – yet I wish
it meant something. I wish it signified.

Repatriation
Scotland 2006

Despite the lifetimes holding us apart,
I hope that something ancient still connects
this land and I, that some lost Celt within
might range about these hills and reminisce –

yet waking in the night, my panicked heart
quails in its open cage, and recollects
the true ancestral home of all its kin:
Eternity. A vacuum. The abyss.

'the timid heart'

the timid heart
would stall the world at springtime
(o time of sap and promise)
its fruitful resolution always near
but never here

the lazy heart
would choose eternal summer
(o time of blueskied shimmer)
applauding as the endless sun deploys
its shallow joys

the doleful heart
would hold the year at autumn
(o time of brittle colour)
when leaves in melancholic reds and browns
descend like frowns

the bitter heart
would suffer none but winter
(o time of frost and stasis)
meeting the bleak and fallow cold with cold
no thaw foretold

the living heart
beats forward the march of seasons
(o time, o ceaseless time)
as though its mortal rhythm might prevail
or seasons fail

Paranoia

The first reaction is a dumb bemusement
charged with startle, as in the opening lurch
of an earthquake when your senses, jolted, spike
their dials to max before the sense is grasped
of what just happened. Sudden silent dark,
the background mumble of the ageing fridge
and central heating gone, a curtain dropped
mid-act across the TV drama you were looking at
that's left a jangling after-image in your eyes.

Is it just us? you call out to the house,
then shuffle feelingly towards the kitchen
where flames and candles are, and as you place
those tapered hopes on saucers, see how little light
in actual fact they give, there's something else:
an edgy indignation starts to prickle,
as though your evening were a pair of wrestling pups –
both harmless and endearing – that some anxious fool
just threw cold water over. What a nerve! You glare
resentfully at the ceiling's unlit bulbs,
slouch to the sofa where you'll wait it out.

You sit. The quiet's big. The lights are stubborn.
They don't come on; they don't come on; they don't come on;
and hours in, you're fretted by the questions
skulking in the darkest corners of the room:
like whether it's such a bright idea to keep
the kindling hatchet hanging up so plainly there
behind the unlocked woodshed door; and where
that man from down the street – the one
who never smiles or cedes a courteous inch
of pavement when your morning transits graze –
just where he might be going as he passes
the bars of your low unlockable front gate
for the third time; and why it seems your restless hand
might take its ease if only it could settle
on something with a bit of heft to hold?

54

The assessment

Your sentiments are balanced on the cusp
of artlessness and risibility
he noted in the margin, in red ink.

At lunch, the fortune cookie said: *The one*
who says it can't be done should not disturb
the one who's doing it – which didn't seem

to capture it exactly. On the street,
a tram let off its bell, then bombed away
to overscore the ruled lines of its rails.

View from a window

the birds pass –
the robin and the finch, the sparrow and the crow
they come, they go

the hours pass –
in carnal cells their winkling fingers soon unlock
they tick, they tock

the hurts pass –
as do the joys; in joint or alternating reign
they wax, they wane

the clues pass –
these smatterings, these prickled inklings from the deep
they wake, they sleep

the days pass –
and though I scrape their marrow or refuse them all
they rise, they fall

the birds pass –
wild shadows, gifted that they live but do not know
they come, they go

A small reprieve

When I survey
the brown nest of my hair, I notice that
once more a sneaking cuckoo's crept and spat
some crazy grey

as if to say
Some things are over with, some chances gone.
They won't be back again. Give up. Move on.
Away, away —

and yet today
the hidden root of one white wire disclosed
a silky inch of darkness reimposed:
a gift, a stay

The earthworm

no
one imagines
an earthworm dreaming
it might become a
butterfly or even
just Chuang-
Tzu

few
share its
urge to fashion
finer dirt from dirt,
to pass what
it passes
through

in
the ground
encompassing what's left
of life's green surge
and ebb, what's
left of
you

Conception

Go back to where it all begins:
ten million universes hang
their half-made heads, their half-built wings
as chance kicks down their scaffolding –

> *in vast percentages of doubt*
> *you are the one who comes about*

So whether you set this life alight
(that comes unbidden, goes despite)
or snap your thews against its weight,
recall: at dawn, at noon, at night –

> *no choice is made, no balance weighed*
> *there is no need to be afraid*

A minute's silence

(i.m. Simon Wake, 1961-2008)

We stand encircled at the stony Y
where road and gravelled track connect; beyond,
a twisting path away and up the hill;
beneath, the cold intransigence of ground.
Some gesture, then, some fleeting monument
of silence, yes? And so our quiet makes
a gap the restless morning wants to fill:

a cow lows across the carse; a pause;
she lows again. A startled pheasant grinds
his rusty gears, then clatters to ascension.
The grimy sheep's observances produce
erratic bleats of woolly liturgy;
even the distant knots of trees are loud
in farewell *kyries* of autumn colour.

In absence, hurt. In stillness, eloquence.
The speechless minute passes. Words return
and turn themselves to memories of you.
Our murmurs rise and join the clear-skied morning's
gentle mass of sound; the vocal blackbird
tells us, Simon, whatever silence is
it isn't what you were. Or where you are.

Summer morning why

because
the summer mornings squire in the long, long days
while winter light came timidly, coaxed from its white bed

because
the coffee packet breathes a languid chocolate sigh
conquering the tea and its brisk ascetic tannins

because
the dog casts her bounding optimism out
to the dawn, the cool trees leaning in to taste it

because
the sky seals its flysheet taut to the horizons
the sun's burner swelling the billow of its dome

because
today's like every other day, a one-off chance,
a radiance leaking from routine's starched cuffs

The gift

Sometimes the recompense arrives
so far ahead of what you'll give
that you will fail to recognise
the reciprocity, the love

that circles in the universe:
this life a grace advanced, its knack
to meet requital with its cause –
the offering up, the giving back.

Marchmont Road

Above the tarmacked voids that breach
the ranks of tenements, a reach

of sky to which the day has lent
a calibrated gradient

of northern blue. Along the road
the pelt of antlike cars is slowed:

a hearse in mirror-faultless gloss
precedes its cavalcade of loss,

and while this dark skein passes, I
cast out for where its gist might lie...

Stop it. No moment *must* encore
itself in some pert metaphor.

Suspend that distanced commentary.
Take a deep breath. Now *be* here. Be.